The Pocket Guide to
Scilly Birds

Nigel Hudson & Danni Borrett

Introduction

The aim of this book is to show the common birds that occur in Scilly – but which birds should be given the category 'common'? It certainly isn't the species that you would call 'common' in mainland Britain. We have only had six sightings of Magpie, and there has never been a Nuthatch! So you won't find either of those in this book, or a number of others you might expect, but for more on this see below.

Should we include the likes of Little Bunting or Cory's Shearwater? These are rare birds in Britain but we now get Little Buntings in Scilly every year and Cory's Shearwater has sometimes been seen in flocks of 100 or more just off the islands, with over 2000 occurring in 1999. But Little Buntings virtually only occur in October and the only chance of seeing Cory's Shearwater is to go out on a specialist boat trip.

Taking all this into account we decided on the simple criterion of selecting the birds you are most likely to see whilst on holiday in Scilly.

Photographs

The photographs have all been taken in Scilly and we believe they are some of the best taken anywhere in Britain. We have tried to pick photographs that show the birds as they are commonly seen, so not necessarily the bird out in the open, but maybe in flight, or sitting on the water. That said, we have also inserted a number of full page shots which we think deserve a special place, and we have also included one or two birds which are not exactly common but the photograph is so good we couldn't leave it out.

Scilly, despite being under 1600 hectares (6.2 square miles) has the largest number of species seen in any county in Britain, and probably for any location in Europe with over 425 species having been seen to date. Luckily for this book about 220 of these are vagrants that have come from America, the Middle East and even Asia and they have only occurred a handful of times. Another 100 or so species occur most years but only one or two birds are usually seen in the spring or autumn migration periods. So that leaves us with the 104 common species covered in this book.

Bird Information

Birds are presented in the modern order which reflects their evolutionary relationships. Swans were one of the earliest species to evolve and hence are at the start of the book followed by ducks and game birds and this continues through to the most recently evolved group, the perching birds known as passerines.

For every species there is a brief description of the bird with the important features in **bold**. If your bird does not have these features then maybe you have got the wrong species! Remember with certain species there will be different plumages for males and females and in autumn young birds may not have developed their full adult plumage. This is particularly true of gulls and terns, with gulls taking from 2-4 years to become full adults.

When a bird is described as small/medium/large it is based on the type of bird: a medium wader is Redshank, a medium gull is Lesser Black-backed Gull, whilst a medium garden/woodland bird is Blackbird.

Then follows **_Best place to see_**, which gives the habitat where the species will be found. These include wetland, woodland, heathland etc. Wetlands (which are often partly saline) include Great Pool and Abbey Pool on Tresco, Lower and Higher Moors (especially Porth Hellick Pool) on St Mary's and Bryher Pool. Muddy fringes occur on all of these wetland locations. Woodland is found mainly on Tresco and St Mary's whereas heathland, often in conjunction with coastal grassland, is found on all the inhabited islands. Another important habitat is the shelter belt hedge, such as *pittosporum*, that is planted to protect cultivated fields from wind damage.

Some birds are best seen from boat trips. For example, Puffins breed on Annet so take a 'Shearwater Special' to see them. Or you can be more adventurous and take a pelagic (open sea) trip that will go out about 10 kilometres from St Mary's. You should see lots of different Gulls, Storm-petrels and Shearwaters, and other marine life such as Basking Sharks, Sun Fish and Dolphins. The pelagics run in the summer months usually leaving early evening.

Next comes **Best time to see:** giving the main months or sometimes a season such as spring/autumn. If you think you have seen a bird out of the period mentioned then look again. It is true that birds do occur 'out of time' but only very rarely. You will NOT get a Cuckoo in winter (it will be in Africa), and Redwing should not occur in summer (they will be breeding in Scandinavia)

We continue with **Numbers:** which tells you how many birds you could expect to see together. Is it likely to be on its own, or in small parties feeding on the shore, or in large flocks or 'rafts' sitting on the sea? It could help you decide that those 200 black seabirds swimming in The Roads are going to be Shags not Cormorants. For breeding birds the approximate number of pairs is given.

Finally, if appropriate, there is a section giving **Similar species:** which tell you of others that can occur; but bear in mind they are not *likely* to be seen. Always assume it is the common species unless the key identification features just don't seem to be there. Then you can look at the photographs in the back of the book where some of these less likely species are shown.

Birds you don't see

Although Scilly has the largest list of species for any location in Europe it is also remarkable for the common birds that have never occurred here, or are extremely rare. For example Scilly has never been graced with Nuthatch, Lesser Spotted Woodpecker or Willow Tit. Magpie has only occurred six times (although one has been resident on St Martin's since 2001), Jay only seven times and Green Woodpecker only twice. Compare that with the 20 occurrences of Blackpoll Warbler all the way from America or 30 or more Red-rumped Swallows from the Mediterranean and beyond. So if you wonder why Rook, Treecreeper, Yellowhammer, Tawny Owl and others are not included it is because they are uncommon on the islands. If you want to know more about the relative abundance of birds over here then the yearly Review published by the Isles of Scilly Bird Group is available *www.scillybirding.co.uk* and a comprehensive book covering every species that has ever occurred is being published in late 2006, entitled 'Essential Guide to Birds of the Isles of Scilly' *www.scillybirdbook.co.uk*.

Nigel Hudson has lived in Scilly since 2001 and is 'semi-retired' although writing books is fast becoming his day job! He is active with the local bird scene via the Isles of Scilly Bird Group, and is Bird Recorder for the islands. His partner, Danni Borrett is Membership Secretary to the bird group and brings her lay-out and typesetting expertise to the design of this pocket guide. The fantastic photographs were provided by restaurant owner Bryan Thomas who has lived on the islands since 1984.

Nigel Hudson and Danni Borrett
Post Office Flat, St Mary's
Email: nigel-hudson@tiscali.co.uk or dannibee@tiscali.co.uk

Mute Swan

This well known swan has an **orange bill** and black near the eye. In Scilly it sometimes occurs in a different habitat to mainland Britain. Although still seen on freshwater pools, it can also be seen swimming elegantly along sheltered bays a few metres offshore.

Best place to see: Freshwater such as Great Pool Tresco, Porth Hellick Pool St Mary's and Big Pool St Agnes, but also in sheltered bays such as Old Town St Mary's, especially in winter.

Best time to see: Seen throughout the year. Cygnets only seen in the later summer months.

Numbers: Usually in pairs or family parties of up to six birds but with occasional parties of 20-25 birds, mainly on Great Pool Tresco. Between two and five pairs breed.

Similar species: The wild *Whooper Swan* (page 120) occasionally occurs in Scilly but only from October and through the winter. Look for bright yellow bill with black tip.

"I hope I've been cleared for take-off!"

Canada Goose

A large grey goose with a black neck and **white chinstrap**.
Best place to see: Freshwater pools, especially Great Pool Tresco.
Best time to see: All year round.
Numbers: Usually seen in small groups and in recent years a party of up to six has frequented Great Pool Tresco.
Similar species: Wild geese such as *White-fronted* and *Brent* (page 120) occasionally occur in winter.

Common Shelduck

A large, mainly white, duck with **black head and neck** and russet breast band. The **bright red bill** is very prominent.

Best place to see: Freshwater pools such as Porth Hellick St Mary's and sheltered bays especially Porth Killier St Agnes.

Best time to see: All year round but highest numbers are from April-July when most birds leave the islands to moult. It is thought that their moulting grounds are in Bridgwater Bay Somerset. They return here in October.

Numbers: Typically seen in small parties from two to six birds with maximum numbers around 25. Approximately 20 pairs breed across all the islands.

Gadwall

A typical duck with mainly grey plumage and a **black rear**.

Best place to see: Freshwater pools on all islands.

Best time to see: All year round with maximum numbers in September and October.

Numbers: Normally seen in scattered groups of around 10-15 birds with a resident population of about 40 birds split across the islands. An autumn influx boosts numbers to 50-70 birds. Around 15 pairs breed here.

Teal

A **small** duck with red and green head (male only) and prominent **cream rear**. The female is less colourful with a mainly brown body.
Best place to see: Freshwater pools on all islands.
Best time to see: Mainly September to November with a small over-wintering population.
Numbers: Can be seen in concentrations of over 100 birds in autumn especially October, reducing to 30-40 during the winter. Numbers reduce drastically from March to five to six birds. Note: only one or two birds are ever seen during the summer.

Mallard

The standard British duck! Medium to large duck with **iridescent green head** (male) a **bright yellow bill** and prominent white flash in the tail.

Best place to see: Freshwater pools and sheltered bays across all islands. In Scilly the Mallard is often see in pairs and small groups, off beaches such as Porthloo and Porth Mellon and just off the quay, all on St Mary's.

Best time to see: All year round.

Numbers: Often seen in flocks of 10-30 birds and total counts on Great Pool Tresco can exceed 200, especially in October. This increase is due to young birds being introduced on Tresco in early autumn. Approximately 30-60 pairs breed across all islands.

Pochard

Medium sized duck with grey body and **russet head** (male).

Best place to see: Freshwater pools on all islands but especially Great Pool Tresco.

Best time to see: Mainly in winter with a few birds remaining through the summer.

Numbers: Normally seen in ones and twos although, very rarely, 10 or more birds can be seen in the winter months only. One pair has bred on Great Pool Tresco in recent years.

Tufted Duck

A medium sized **black and white** duck, with males showing a **drooping crest** (the tuft) in the breeding season.

Best place to see: Freshwater especially Great Pool Tresco and Porth Hellick Pool St Mary's.

Best time to see: All year round.

Numbers: Ones and twos. Breeding has been attempted in recent years.

Red-legged Partridge

A medium sized game bird with prominent **white face** and black highwayman's mask. Has a fat body with light brown back and **boldly striped flanks**, and in good views the red legs can be seen.

Best place to see: Main populations are on Tresco and St Mary's but it has now spread to Bryher and St Martin's. Often seen feeding in ploughed fields, usually keeping to the edges, but when disturbed it runs at high speed into cover.

Best time to see: All year round.

Numbers: This partridge was introduced to the islands in 1993 and has become established such that small parties of around 10 birds are often seen. It is thought there are about 30 breeding pairs but numbers are 'muddied' by yearly introductions.

Pheasant

This well-known, large game bird was introduced on Tresco in the late 19th century. It is often first noticed when a **loud croaking squawk** is heard. The male is **unmistakeable** (see photo), while the female has an overall dull brown plumage.
Best place to see: Mainly in cultivated fields on Tresco with smaller numbers on other inhabited islands.
Best time to see: All year round.
Numbers: Usually in small parties of up to 20 birds. Birds are introduced each year on Tresco leading to larger numbers being seen in autumn, with sometimes as many as 200 being counted across the whole island.

Golden Pheasant

A **stunning** bird once seen **never forgotten**! (see photo). Unfortunately once again the female falls short in the beauty stakes being the usual dull brown plumage.
Best place to see: Abbey Drive Tresco where a small pen holds introduced birds whilst roaming birds will be seen in the vicinity, often scratching around under rhododendron bushes along the path. Also around Rowsefield Tresco, especially in the spring.
Best time to see: All year round.
Numbers: Usually seen in singles with total numbers probably no more than 10. May occasionally breed but this relies on introductions.

Great Northern Diver

Sometimes confused with a Cormorant but heavier and bulkier. See the strong neck, heavy **dagger-shaped bill** and **off-white front** to the neck (winter plumage). Occasionally stays into early summer when traces of its breeding plumage, black-and-white patterned back and small white collar on the neck, will be seen.

Best place to see: Always on the sea, never on rocks. Favoured spots are Crow Sound between St Mary's and St Martin's and in Smith Sound out towards Annet and the Western Rocks.

Best time to see: Numbers build up from late October to a peak around the year-end, then reducing to the beginning of May. Hardly ever seen between mid-May and the end of September.

Numbers: Usually in ones and twos with occasional groups of up to 10 birds in mid-winter.

Fulmar

Superficially like a small to medium sized gull, but actually related to the albatrosses with which it shares the ability to **glide effortlessly on stiff wings**. Note pure white head and body and **grey wings** with **no black tips**.

Best place to see: As you pass between the islands, especially around those that are uninhabited. Breeds on Annet, Round Island, Northern and Western Rocks, and also on the Eastern Isles.

Best time to see: At any time of year, especially late summer and early autumn but almost never in late October and November.

Numbers: Generally in ones and twos and sometimes up to five, but with breeding pairs increasing to over 150 it could well be seen in larger numbers in the coming years.

Manx Shearwater

A medium sized shearwater, with an **all over plain dark back and head** contrasting with a white underside.

Best place to see: Take a 'Shearwater Special' trip on a summer's evening and see a 'raft of birds' sitting on the water off Annet, waiting to go in to their nests at night. Also a few occasionally shear past headlands such as Peninnis St Mary's, a few hundred metres offshore.

Best time to see: From May to August with peak numbers in June and July.

Numbers: The rafts off Annet can number up to 300 birds, but otherwise typically four or five birds will be seen together when flying past headlands. Although very difficult to count it is thought that there are around 200-300 pairs breeding in Scilly, making the islands *Regionally Significant* for this species with the only other breeding colony in England being on Lundy Island.

Similar species: *Great Shearwater* (page 121) which can be see on pelagic trips.

European Storm-petrel

A very small seabird looking like a House Martin, with an all black body and **white rump**.

Best place to see: Normally only seen near the islands at dusk when it flies into its nesting burrows on Annet or Round Island and even then can be very difficult to see. However an autumn pelagic trip (see page 4) may be more productive when birds can be seen at sea a few kilometres offshore.

Best time to see: Late May to end of August.

Numbers: On a pelagic trip you can often see 10 to 20 birds in loose groups feeding around the boat. However the total numbers breeding in Scilly are estimated at over 1500 pairs making the islands *Internationally Important* for this species, and Scilly remains the only breeding colony in England.

Gannet

A **very large** seabird with **gleaming white wings** and body except for the **black wing tips** extending to almost half the wing length. Heavy light blue bill. Beware of juvenile and young birds, which show a variety of patchy grey colours but the 'flying cross' shape remains. Also note the **spectacular dive with wings pulled back** as it plunges into the sea to catch fish.

Best place to see: Over the sea anywhere around the islands, coming closer to the shore in rough weather.

Best time to see: Present all year, but largest numbers in September to November and much lower numbers through the spring.

Numbers: Usually ones and twos are seen when close to the islands, but passage past headlands can give counts of 50 or more birds in an hour. Sometimes an autumn pelagic trip will come across a flock of up to 100 birds frantically feeding over a shoal of mackerel – a spectacular sight.

Cormorant

That black bird sitting like a thin-necked duck on the sea will be a Shag or a Cormorant but which one? Although Shag is much more common there are still plenty of Cormorants, with their generally **paler throat patch** and **heavier bill** that smoothly joins on to the head (compare with Shag, next page).

Best place to see: All round the islands at sea, and sitting in small numbers on rocky outcrops. Very occasionally can be seen on Porth Hellick Pool St Mary's where it may fish for eels.

Best time to see: All year round.

Numbers: Usually in ones and twos, maybe up to six, but *never* in large flocks (compare with Shag). Around 50 pairs breed in Scilly, mainly on the uninhabited rocky outcrops.

Shag

Slightly smaller than Cormorant and with a much **finer bill** that looks like it is stuck on to the head with glue – one quick snap and it will come off! In summer it has a **quiff** on its head – the 'shag' – that gives the bird its name.

Best place to see: All round the islands at sea, and sitting in groups on rocky outcrops.

Best time to see: All year round.

Numbers: Can be seen swimming and feeding in ones and twos but will form large groups of 100 or more birds on rocky outcrops and even larger rafts of up to 1000 birds can sometimes be seen sitting on the water in The Roads or Crow Sound, with other birds flying in to join them alighting on the edge of the growing raft. Over 1000 pairs breed on the islands, a *Nationally Important* proportion of the UK population.

"Did someone say FISH?"

Grey Heron

The standard heron, with **grey plumage**, a mainly white neck, and a long dagger-shaped bill. Adult birds have long, black eyebrows. In flight its huge, slow flapping, gently curved wings are easily picked out.

Best place to see: Highest counts are on Tresco and along Tresco Channel, but can be seen on any island or rocky outcrop, or on freshwater pools such as Lower Moors and Porth Hellick St Mary's.

Best time to see: All year round, with numbers increasing from July to October as migrant birds pass through the islands.

Numbers: Usually in small groups from one to ten birds, but occasionally up to 30 birds come together.

Purple Heron

Similar to the far more common Grey Heron, but its **reddish-brown neck** and darker (purple) grey plumage help the identification.
Best place to see: Reed beds on Tresco or St Mary's.
Best time to see: Spring, May to June inclusive.
Numbers: One, or very occasionally two, in any year. It is rare but regular in Scilly.

Little Egret

An **all white** heron, with long black bill and legs and amazingly bright **yellow feet**!

Best place to see: Best seen on Great Pool Tresco but often sitting on rocks along Tresco Channel, and occasionally feeding in rocky pools along the shores of any island.

Best time to see: Highest numbers occur from July to October with a peak in late September and early October. Less likely to be seen during winter and spring, although this may be more apparent than real, as birds disperse to the outer islands to feed, before returning to Tresco for the summer.

Numbers: Groups of 10-30 birds can be seen on favoured sites whilst singles occur when feeding on the shoreline. First seen here in 1955, numbers have increased to around 35 birds, part of a major expansion of this species in Britain. However breeding has not taken place so far, despite the seemingly ideal conditions that exist around the islands.

"Yellow is this season's colour you know!"

Sparrowhawk

A medium sized bird of prey with mainly grey plumage in adults (see photo) but we often get immature birds which have a brown toned back. The underside is **barred.** In flight the **rounded** wing tips, typical of hawks, help differentiate it from Kestrel. When seen well the yellow eye is distinctive.

Best place to see: All over the wooded areas on St Mary's and Tresco.

Best time to see: All year although *very rare* in the summer months.

Numbers: Usually seen as a single bird soaring over woodland, or if you are lucky chasing its unlucky sparrow prey.

Kestrel

A small to medium falcon with **rusty brown back** and pointed wings (typical of falcons). Can often be seen drifting on the wind along cliff edges, or **hovering** motionless, head down, looking for prey.

Best place to see: Anywhere but especially over short grassy areas along the coastal footpaths such as Peninnis headland or near the Golf Course St Mary's.

Best time to see: All year round.

Numbers: Usually seen singly, or occasionally in pairs.

Similar species: The slightly smaller *Merlin* (page 121) can be confused with Kestrel.

Peregrine

A medium sized falcon with a fast strong flight often on straight outstretched wings. Note the grey **cigar-shaped body** and **black moustache** just below the eye. (see photo) When seen well the **yellow legs** and feet stand out.

Best place to see: Around the Eastern Isles where it breeds. It can often be seen sitting out in a prominent position looking for prey, but its hunting flights can take it quickly across to any of the islands.

Best time to see: All year round.

Numbers: Normally a single bird is seen, but a pair has successfully bred on Eastern Isles for the last few years and can be seen with the young in July and August before they disperse, presumably over to Cornwall.

Water Rail

Maybe best described as 'like a Moorhen in shape' but smaller, with brown plumage, grey face and a much longer, more **pointed**, distinct **red bill**. Often secretive, keeping in reeds, but occasionally feeding along the reed edge and then running quickly across open water to the next reedy edge. If when in Lower or Higher Moors St Mary's you hear a **loud squeal like a stuck pig** – then you have just heard a Water Rail!

Best place to see: Reedy margins such as found around Lower and Higher Moors St Mary's, or Great Pool Tresco.

Best time to see: All year round although very rarely seen from May to July.

Numbers: Usually only a single bird will be seen. Water Rail possibly breeds in Scilly but its secretive nature, and the fact it will only breed in the middle of a wet reed bed, makes this difficult to prove.

Common Moorhen

A dumpy dark chicken-like bird with white tail flash and **yellow bill** with a **red shield**, make it unmistakeable. Look for its strutting gait with the **white tail flicking** constantly. The cream line along the edge of the wing (see photo) is another prominent feature.

Best place to see: Always near water, especially in short grassy fields such as those at the west end of Great Pool Tresco. Also at Lower and Higher Moors St Mary's.

Best time to see: All year round with a peak in late autumn.

Numbers: Twos and threes will be seen swimming on freshwater pools, with larger groups of up to 20 birds assembling on the surrounding fields. Occasionally larger flocks of up to 50 birds may gather, especially in cold weather when they come out in the open to feed. About 20-30 pairs breed here.

Common Coot

In some ways similar to Common Moorhen but the **pure white bill and shield** are distinctive.

Best place to see: Swimming on freshwater such as Great Pool Tresco and Porth Hellick Pool St Mary's. Also seen on the grassy fields adjacent to the pools.

Best time to see: All year round with a peak in late autumn.

Numbers: Swimming flocks from 20 to over 100 birds can be seen on Great Pool Tresco, with smaller numbers elsewhere. About 15-20 pairs breed here.

Oystercatcher

One of the most obvious, and larger, shore birds in Scilly with its **black and white** plumage, long **straight orange bill**, and its **piercing call** *'kleepa-kleepa'*.

Best place to see: Probing along sandy shorelines, and into seaweed pools.

Best time to see: All year round.

Numbers: Often seen in groups of up to 20 or more birds, loosely spaced along the shoreline. About 150 pairs breed here and so there could be over 400 birds spread over the whole archipelago in the period after the breeding season i.e. late August to October.

"Flying free!"

Ringed Plover

A small wader, with **distinctive head pattern** – black mask, white collar and black breast band (see photo) – and a **small orange bill** tipped with black. Quite a **chunky** little bird.

Best place to see: Along sandy shores and small rock pools on any island but prefers the quieter beaches with less disturbance.

Best time to see: All year round but numbers greatest during autumn migration (September-October) and spring migration (late February-early March).

Numbers: During migration can often be seen in parties of up to 50 birds, with maybe 200 or more around all the islands. In summer it is usually only seen in twos and threes, with about 30 pairs breeding in the archipelago.

Similar species: The very similar *Little Ringed Plover* (page 121) may occasionally be seen in spring.

Dotterel

A small to medium sized brown wader with a **distinct white eyebrow** (supercilium) which extends down behind the head and neck. Can be **remarkably tame**, allowing approach to a metre or less, as it hunkers down in the heather.

Best place to see: On open heather areas such as within the Golf Course or near the airport on St Mary's, on Castle Down Tresco or Shipman Head Bryher. They can easily disappear by tucking down low between the patches of heather and rock. When finally disturbed they may prefer to scuttle away rather than fly.

Best time to see: Only on migration, in spring mid-April to mid-May, or in autumn from September to October.

Numbers: Usually ones and twos, sometimes in small groups of up to five birds.

Golden Plover

A medium sized wader with **speckled golden brown** plumage and a small **beady black eye**. In summer plumage a black face and breast are sported.

Best place to see: Often seen in ploughed fields especially those near Telegraph St Mary's or on Browarth St Agnes. Also on short grass such as at the Golf Course or Airport St Mary's.

Best time to see: From September through to early spring.

Numbers: Often in small groups of five to ten birds, occasionally up to 30 birds.

Similar species: The *Grey Plover* (page 121), which of course has a greyer plumage, could be confused with Golden Plover.

Lapwing

A medium sized wader with **black and white head pattern** (see photo) and a **crest**. The back is plain green with a white belly. In flight its very **rounded wing tips** are distinctive, often accompanied by a far-carrying '*pee-wit*' call. (Peewit is a local name in some parts of Britain).

Best place to see: On ploughed fields such as at Telegraph and Normandy St Mary's.

Best time to see: Mainly in winter from October through to February.

Numbers: Small parties of two to five birds with occasional groups of 20 or more.

Sanderling

A small wader running like a **clockwork toy** along the tideline, usually in groups of at least 20-30 birds. Has a cold grey white plumage and **black legs**.

Best place to see: Sandy beaches such as at Porth Mellon and Porthloo St Mary's, Lawrence's Bay and Par Beach St Martin's and Periglis St Agnes.

Best time to see: All year round but numbers are much lower from mid-May to mid-July. Peak counts occur in late October with many birds remaining through the winter months.

Numbers: Usually in groups of 20 or more birds, sometimes as many as 150 to 200.

Purple Sandpiper

A small wader with a dark grey plumage, **lack of markings on dark grey head**, and a white belly with lines of darker feathers showing. **Orange base to bill** going darker towards the tip.

Best place to see: Behind the sea-wall at the Mermaid Pub on St Mary's or other tide-line rocks such as around the Garrison St Mary's or on Porth Killier St Agnes. Often seen where the waves are just breaking, somehow gripping the rocks and feeding quickly as the wave recedes.

Best time to see: A winter visitor from late October through to early May.

Numbers: Small groups of around five birds but their numbers seem to have decreased in recent years although it is too early to say whether this is a permanent change.

Curlew Sandpiper

An elegant small wader with **slightly down-curved bill**. Can be confused with Dunlin (see opposite) but note its clean white belly (Dunlin only has this in the winter) and sometimes a coral pink suffusion of colour on the throat and breast. In flight its **white rump** will always separate it from Dunlin.

Best place to see: Sandy and rock-strewn beaches such as Porth Mellon and Porthloo on St Mary's or Periglis and Porth Killier St Agnes.

Best time to see: As an autumn migrant it comes through the islands in the last week of August until the second week of October. Very rarely a lone bird may pass through in late May.

Numbers: Usually singly but occasionally up to five birds may occur.

Dunlin

A dumpy **nondescript** small wader with brown back and a **slightly down-curved bill** but never as much as in Curlew Sandpiper (see opposite). Although bird books will show Dunlin with a black belly patch this is only on breeding birds which very rarely occur here. **Feeds methodically**, with no theatrical gestures, among the seaweed on sandy beaches.

Best place to see: Sandy and seaweed laden beaches such as Porth Mellon St Mary's or Periglis St Agnes.

Best time to see: A short-lived spring passage in the middle of May, then none until early July when it becomes more common through to September. Numbers then decrease but occasional sightings occur during the winter months.

Numbers: Usually seen in small parties of five to ten birds, but during the August-October autumn migration this can increase to 20-30 birds.

Jack Snipe

A medium sized, generally brown, wader with **cream stripes** on face and back. It has a fairly long bill, about 1 1/2 times the head length, compared with Common Snipe (see opposite). Frequents freshwater pools where its comic **bobbing up-and-down** as though on a spring, will catch the eye.

Best place to see: Freshwater pool margins especially at Lower Moors and Porth Hellick St Mary's.

Best time to see: Absent from May through to September at which time an autumn passage occurs. One or two can remain through the year-end and in to April.

Numbers: Rarely more than one or two, and tends to keep itself to itself, even when there are two along one pool margin.

Common Snipe

A large, generally brown, wader with **cream stripes** on face and back. It has a **long straight bill**, at over twice the head length, which is comparatively longer than that of Jack Snipe (see opposite).

Best place to see: Freshwater pools especially Lower Moors and Porth Hellick St Mary's and Great Pool Tresco.

Best time to see: October to December with smaller numbers through to April. Very unlikely to be seen from May to July, after which numbers start building up.

Numbers: In the early winter period can be seen in large groups of 20-70 or more birds, standing motionless amongst the reed edges, and often seen in small groups rather than individual birds.

Whimbrel

A large, generally brown, wader with a long **down-curved bill** (about 1 1/2 times the head length). Its smaller size and the cream **crown stripe**, along the top of the head, separate it from Curlew. Gives a **far-carrying call** – 'pu hu hu hu hu hu'.

Best place to see: Nearly always near the sea edge, either on the rocks or along the seaweed shore. In spring it is seen on short turf such as the cricket pitches on St Agnes and St Martin's.

Best time to see: A definite peak is the last week of April and first week of May after which only a few birds are seen through to October. Very rarely seen in winter.

Numbers: The spring passage can see groups of 20-50 birds but at other times only ones and twos will be seen.

Curlew

A **very large**, generally brown, wader with a **very long down-curved bill**, over twice the head length. Often first noticed by its melancholic call – '*cour-leew*' – from which it gets its name.

Best place to see: Always near the sea edge, often walking slowly over the rocks, and sometimes along the seaweed shore.

Best time to see: From July to September and a smaller peak at the start of the year.

Numbers: In the peak season it can be seen in flocks of 60-100 birds, but ones and twos can be seen in any month of the year.

Redshank

A medium sized, generally brown, wader with **red legs** and a **straight red bill** (darker at the tip).

Best place to see: Freshwater pools especially Porth Hellick St Mary's and Great Pool Tresco, and also on beaches feeding along the water's edge.

Best time to see: All year round, but with peak numbers from July to October. Very rare from mid-April to end of June.

Numbers: Usually in ones and twos but groups of 10 or more birds can be seen on Great Pool Tresco in autumn.

Similar species: The *Bar-tailed Godwit* (page 122) is similar but larger, longer legged and has a proportionately longer bill.

Greenshank

A large, generally light grey, wader with **green legs** and a green-grey bill – with the **hint of an upward curve**. Its far-carrying **three- note call** – '*tchew-tew-tew*' – is often heard as it takes off in flight.

Best place to see: Freshwater pools especially Porth Hellick St Mary's and Great Pool Tresco, and 'up to its ankles' feeding along the water's edge of any beach.

Best time to see: All year round with peak numbers from July to October, although they are much less common in May and June.

Numbers: Usually in ones, twos and threes but groups of 20 or more birds can be seen on Great Pool Tresco in autumn.

Common Sandpiper

A medium sized wader, with grey-buff back and pure white belly with a **white epaulette** at the shoulder (see photo). Often **rocks its body** (pivoting at the legs) as it lands, and as it feeds. Has a characteristic flight where the **wings are held stiff** and only beat downward below the bodyline.

Best place to see: Rocky boulders and sheltered beaches, occasionally on freshwater margins such as at Porth Hellick Pool St Mary's and Great Pool Tresco.

Best time to see: From April to early October.

Numbers: Usually seen in ones and twos, although counts in August may rise to ten.

Similar species: Both *Green Sandpiper* and *Wood Sandpiper* (page 122) are similar in size, but neither have the epaulette.

Turnstone

A medium sized wader, with a cryptic and quite variable plumage. Has a russet coloured back, an almost **black breast plate** and a plain white belly. Its **orange legs** stand out. Often seen on the seashore feeding near seaweed and rocky pools where it uses its bill to poke under seaweed and pebbles to find food – the 'turner of stones'. Can be **quite tame**.

Best place to see: Sheltered seashores with pebbles and seaweed. On St Mary's try Town Beach and over the sea wall near the Mermaid, whilst Periglis and Porth Killier St Agnes are other good spots.

Best time to see: All year round with an increase during autumn migration from mid-September to early December.

Numbers: Often in feeding flocks of 20 or more birds, scurrying around as the waves come in.

Arctic Skua

The piratical chaser of gulls and terns. Similar to a large gull but more falcon-like with **long pointed wings**, and a long pointed tail, and a **plain brown upper plumage** with white belly. Skuas will chase gulls and terns to make them disgorge their food rather than bother to find some for themselves!

Best place to see: On a pelagic trip (see page 4) a few kilometres out at sea.

Best time to see: From July to October but never in winter. Also a few are seen between the islands in early summer harassing the terns as they arrive to breed.

Numbers: Usually just one.

Great Skua

A very large **robust** brown 'gull' with **white flashes in the wing** – well that's a Great Skua or Bonxie as they are sometimes called.

Best place to see: Out at sea on one of the pelagic trips (see page 4) although occasionally a single bird may fly past a headland such as Peninnis St Mary's or Horse Point St Agnes.

Best time to see: From July to October.

Numbers: Usually just one.

Black-headed Gull

The standard gull on mainland but not quite so common in Scilly. It should be called a **dark brown-headed** gull, as you can see if you look closely, and only in the summer does that dark head appear. In winter the plumage is more blotchy grey around the head. Has a **deep coloured red bill,** sometimes with darker tip.

Best place to see: Any beach but especially those of Porthcressa and Porthloo St Mary's. Also often seen off Morning Point (on the Garrison) St Mary's sitting on the sea.

Best time to see: Comes in three bursts during the year – January, mid-July and mid-October.

Numbers: Usually seen in small groups of three to ten birds feeding along the water's edge. Flocks of birds sitting on offshore rocks or on the water can exceed 50 in number.

"Hope I'll get a black head when I grow up!"

Lesser Black-backed Gull

A medium sized gull which is very common in Scilly, with a **grey back** and **yellow legs**. There is a greater contrast between the grey of the back and the white neck and body in this species compared with Herring Gull (opposite) which has a much paler, silvery grey back.

Best place to see: Just about anywhere except in a bush! Feeding along beaches and on rocks offshore, flying over the inter-island waters, swimming on Porth Hellick St Mary's and other freshwater pools or loafing around on the Golf Course St Mary's.

Best time to see: All year round but much less common in winter.

Numbers: Groups of 50 or more birds are common at any time of year except during winter. With over 3000 breeding pairs in Scilly the islands are of *International Importance* for this species.

Herring Gull

A very common gull in Scilly. A medium to large gull with **silvery grey back** and **pink legs**. Compare with Lesser Black-backed Gull for the contrast shown between the mantle (back) and the neck and body.

Best place to see: The same as Lesser Black-backed Gull, this species can be seen just about anywhere, but with a preference for boulder beaches.

Best time to see: All year round but with an increase in September and October after breeding, combined with autumn migration.

Numbers: Groups of 50 or more are commonly seen, with higher counts of 200-500 birds occurring in October. There are over 900 breeding pairs on the islands.

Great Black-backed Gull

The largest gull in Scilly with a **dark grey back** and **pink legs**. It could be confused with a dark grey example of Lesser Black-backed Gull (which do occur) but note the massive size and the pink legs of Great Black-backed.

Best place to see: Similar again to Lesser Black-backed Gull but maybe less inclined to be seen on grass and more likely to be at sea.

Best time to see: All year round but with an increase in September and October after breeding, combined with autumn migration.

Numbers: Groups of 100 or more birds are common and during the autumn, after breeding, groups of 500 plus may gather together. With around 800 breeding pairs in Scilly the islands are of *National Importance* for this species.

Kittiwake

A small gull with **wing tips** that have been '**dipped in ink**' i.e. with black tips that are the same on the upper and underside of the wing. Has a very clean white head with **beady black eye.** Immatures have a black collar and a black 'V' on each wing, creating a flying 'W' across the back.

Best place to see: Flying over inter-island waters especially in The Roads and Crow Sound. One of the breeding colonies which is easiest to see is at Gimble Porth Tresco with another on Gugh.

Best time to see: All year round.

Numbers: Normally just one or two birds are seen together, but during hard weather birds will fly in from out at sea and loose flocks of 100 to over 1000 may be seen in The Roads and Crow Sound. About 250 pairs breed around the islands.

Sandwich Tern

Terns are the 'swallows of the sea'. Their pointed wing tips and graceful flight separates them from the gulls. Sandwich Tern is the largest tern seen in Scilly and has a **shaggy black head** and **black bill with a cream tip**. Its **raucous call** *'skee-rick'* draws your attention to these birds in flight.

Best place to see: Flying over inter-island waters especially The Roads and Crow Sound.

Best time to see: Throughout April the Sandwich Tern is the commonest tern in Scilly waters. However its highest numbers occur from July to end September.

Numbers: Usually seen in ones or twos. Small parties of up to 10-20 birds are commonly seen and groups of up to 100 birds are not unusual.

Common Tern

A medium sized tern with **long tail streamers** and a **postbox-red bill** with a black tip. They are often seen diving in the water to feed.

Best place to see: Flying over inter-island waters especially The Roads and Crow Sound. Also breeds on Annet and Samson. *NB: The whole of Annet and the breeding area on Samson are protected areas and no human disturbance is allowed in the summer months.*

Best time to see: Birds arrive towards the end of April and depart by the end of September.

Numbers: Small parties of three to ten birds will be seen away from the breeding areas. Loose flocks of 100 plus birds can be seen around North Hill Samson where many of the 80-100 pairs that breed in Scilly are located.

Similar species: The *Arctic Tern* has even longer tail streamers and a crimson bill (page 122).

Guillemot

Like a **small penguin** with dark brown back and head and pure white belly. Has a robust **dagger-shaped black bill**. (See Razorbill on page 66 and photo opposite for the differences). In flight – always low over the water – their cigar-shaped body and very fast **whirring wing-beats** are diagnostic of the Auk family which includes Guillemot, Razorbill and Puffin.

Best place to see: Swimming on inter-island waters and standing on isolated rocky islets.

Best time to see: From mid-March to end July when breeding birds leave the islands. An autumn passage, mainly of birds flying past headlands, occurs in October.

Numbers: From one to four birds swimming on the water, or up to 20 birds when standing on the rocks. Between 150-200 pairs breed on the uninhabited islands of Northern and Western Rocks and Men-a-Vaur.

"Sorry my friend doesn't talk to Razorbills!"

Razorbill

Similar to Guillemot (see previous page) but with **black back** – not dark brown – and **square bill with white flash**; supposedly the shape of a cut-throat razor, hence its name.

Best place to see: Swimming on inter-island waters and standing on isolated rocky islets.

Best time to see: Birds arrive from April to breed on the islands, departing in July with their offspring. An autumn passage occurs in October. In the winter months (especially January and February), it is more common than Guillemot.

Numbers: From one to four birds swimming on the water, or up to 20 birds when standing on the rocks. Nearly 300 pairs breed across many of the uninhabited islands.

Similar species: *Little Auk* (page 123) is similar but about half the size – as small as a Starling.

Puffin

If you don't know what a puffin looks like you haven't been shopping for tea towels, sports shirts and other paraphernalia! Its **clown-like looks** with **brightly coloured bill** are unique. At about 30cm (1 ft) high they are much smaller than Guillemot although many people come here with the belief that they are the same size as a penguin!

Best place to see: Take a seabird trip to Mincarlo in the Northern Rocks or Annet where they breed in the burrows above North East Porth and fly out to sea on feeding trips.

Best time to see: Birds start to return here from the last week of March with good numbers building up by May. Breeding occurs from May to July when they suddenly disappear to return to their winter quarters in the northern oceans.

Numbers: On a typical seabird trip in summer you will see between 10-40 birds. Breeding numbers vary from year to year with a minimum of 60 pairs and up to 100 pairs being present.

Stock Dove

Small **all grey** pigeon with **black outer wings**. Beware of confusion with juvenile Woodpigeon (see opposite).
Best place to see: Mainly up-country on St Mary's and around the Abbey on Tresco.
Best time to see: All year round.
Numbers: Usually seen in ones and twos or small groups of up to ten birds. Although up to five pairs have bred in the past there has been no proven success in the last few years.

Woodpigeon

Mainly grey pigeon with a pink suffusion on the breast and **white neck collar** and **white flash in the wings**. However the juvenile lacks the white collar and could be confused with Stock Dove. Its call is distinctive and can be translated as *'take two cows taffy, take two cows taffy, take two cows taffy, take!'* Say this to yourself with elongated *cows* and short, sharp *taffy's* and you'll be doing a fair impression! Don't confuse with the feral/town pigeons that also occur in Scilly, the main flock being seen in Hugh Town. These birds have a variety of plumages often showing a white rump patch and many birds in the flock being paler than their congeners.
Best place to see: On all the inhabited islands.
Best time to see: All year round.
Numbers: Usually seen in ones or twos although flocks of between 50-100 birds do occur. It is estimated that 100 or more pairs breed here.

Collared Dove

A small pigeon with **pale buff plumage** and fine **black neck-band** with a wedge-shaped tail. It's plaintive repeated '*koo-kooo, koo*' call is often heard.

Best place to see: All over the islands.

Best time to see: All year round.

Numbers: Usually seen in ones or twos although flocks of between 40-80 birds do occur especially in Hugh Town. It is estimated that 60 pairs breed here.

Turtle Dove

A small pigeon with small rounded head and **mottled back** of dark brown feathers with fawn fringes. Has a wedge-shaped tail with pure white outer edges. It has a soothing, rolling call '*prrr-urr*' beloved of poets.

Best place to see: On any island, usually sitting in a ploughed field.

Best time to see: An early summer visitor arriving the last half of April through to mid-June with a few birds seen during autumn migration in September and October.

Numbers: Usually one or two birds.

Cuckoo

Usually picked up by **call**; then look out for a large bird (one-third bigger than a Blackbird) often sitting on a prominent spot such as a rock outcrop, frequently with wings drooped below the body. In flight its **long pointed wings** and **very long tail** could lead to confusion with a bird of prey, but unlike raptors, it does not raise its wings above body level and often lands clumsily.

Best place to see: Coastal areas with short grass and rocky outcrops such as the Garrison or Peninnis Head St Mary's and Wingletang St Agnes.

Best time to see: From mid-April to early August. Never in winter.

Numbers: Usually a single bird is seen. As a breeding species it is declining with no more than 10 pairs in recent years. In Scilly the main host species, in whose nest it will lay a single egg, is Rock Pipit whilst on mainland it is Meadow Pipit.

Kingfisher

You may be lucky to see a Kingfisher perched on a rock or post but often it's a **flash of iridescent blue** and a small bird **whirring low over water** that first catches the eye.
Best place to see: Freshwater pools at Lower and Higher Moors St Mary's but also on sandy beaches such as Porth Hellick St Mary's.
Best time to see: Late summer and autumn, from August to October.
Numbers: Usually just a single bird is seen.

Hoopoe

The Hoopoe's striking pink body with boldly **striped black and white wings** is usually seen on a Mediterranean holiday but in Britain, Scilly is probably the best place to see this spring migrant. On landing it often raises its crest which is pink with black tips. Can also be picked up on call – '*oo-poo-poo-poo*'

Best place to see: Short cropped grass especially near coastal paths and on cricket pitches such as those on St Agnes and St Martin's.

Best time to see: March and April.

Numbers: Usually just a single bird is seen; however Scilly has been graced with at least two or three of these birds in each year of the last decade.

Common Swift

The flying anchor. **All dark** plumage (both above and below) with very **long wings in a perfect crescent** and a forked tail. Flies on stiff wings, which are hardly ever flapped (unlike the Swallow).

Best place to see: Always in the air, it never lands or perches. If a Swift landed on the ground its wings would be too long for it to take off again. Only whilst raising young in the nest (which has to be a decent height above the ground) does a Swift stop flying. They can even sleep on the wing.

Best time to see: From the beginning of May through to mid August.

Numbers: Small groups of two to ten birds are usually seen but flocks of 20 or more are possible. Breeding attempts have been made in the last ten years but the success of these is difficult to assess.

Sand Martin

A small bird with **light brown back**, white belly with **brown throat band** and a shallow fork in the tail. Does not have a white rump, unlike its fellow the House Martin.

Best place to see: Usually over freshwater pools such as Porth Hellick St Mary's and Great Pool Tresco.

Best time to see: Arrives second half of March through to end October. Much less common in June and July.

Numbers: Loose groups of up to 10 birds flying over the water, but occasionally flocks of up to 50 birds may be seen.

House Martin

A small bird with blue-black back, white belly and **white rump**. Has a shallow fork in the tail unlike Swallow (see next page). Can often be heard twittering softly in flight.
Best place to see: Almost anywhere but especially over freshwater pools such as Porth Hellick St Mary's and Great Pool Tresco.
Best time to see: From April through to October but most common in May and June.
Numbers: Loose groups of up to 10 birds with occasional flocks of 50-100.

Swallow

An **elegant** fast flying bird of summer with a blue-black back and white belly which is similar to House Martin, but can be easily differentiated as the Swallow has **very long tail streamers**, a red throat (colour sometimes just appears dark) and the rump is blue-black, not white.

Best place to see: Almost anywhere but especially over freshwater pools such as Porth Hellick St Mary's and Great Pool Tresco.

Best time to see: Spring passage occurs from mid-March to mid-June and autumn passage from August to October, with breeding birds present in mid-summer.

Numbers: Twenty or more birds are common, whilst very large flocks of over 100 birds, especially when coming in to roost, are possible at freshwater sites such as Porth Hellick Pool St Mary's. Flocks of 800-1200 have even been recorded. Between 50 and 100 pairs breed on the islands.

"Well I guess summer's over, time to leave"

Meadow Pipit

A nondescript brown bird, one of the proverbial LBJs (little brown jobs). Has a fine pointed bill (that will prevent confusion with a sparrow at least!) and **dark streaks** on a cream-buff belly. In spring and early summer it can be seen doing a 'parachute' flight, dropping slowly from height whilst calling repeatedly *'peest – peet – peet'*.

Best place to see: Often over coastal grassland or in cultivated fields.

Best time to see: Autumn migration (late September and through October) with a smaller spring influx in March and early April.

Numbers: In fields usually seen in loose groups of up to 10 birds, but there's usually more than you think skulking in furrows and under hedges. Occasionally on a low cut grassy area you may see higher numbers out in the open. One or two pairs have bred in recent years.

Rock Pipit

Another nondescript **brown-grey** bird, more robust than Meadow Pipit with a heavier bill but sharing with it a strutting walk.

Best place to see: Much more a bird of coastal edges compared to Meadow Pipit and can often be found feeding on and around large boulders on the beach, and catching flies on seaweed strewn shores. Actually our most widespread bird in Scilly, being seen in 84 per cent of the 1km squares that cover the islands.

Best time to see: All year round.

Numbers: Walking round the rocky shores of any island you will see Rock Pipits at regular intervals. They will be seen in ones and twos but at the end of your walk you have probably seen over 30. It is estimated that 350 pairs breed here making the islands of *National Importance* for this species.

Grey Wagtail

Seeing this elegant wagtail flash past with its **grey back** and **yellow underparts**, many would say it is wrongly named as the yellow stands out. But then what would we call the Yellow Wagtail? It has the **longest tail** of all the wagtails.

Best place to see: Normally near freshwater, so around the edges of pools such as Lower and Higher Moors St Mary's, or up at Newford Duck Pond St Mary's, as well as at Simpson's Field at the western end of Great Pool Tresco.

Best time to see: September through to April. Very rare to non-existent during the summer months.

Numbers: Usually seen singly or occasionally two together.

Similar species: *Yellow Wagtail* (page 123) is similar but has a greenish yellow back.

Pied/White Wagtail

A small **black and white** wagtail. On mainland Britain the Pied form (with black back) is commoner but over here we have more of the White form (see photo) which has a grey back. Often wags its long tail – what a surprise! As it flies listen out for its long thin call – *'tchis-sik'*.

Best place to see: On sandy beaches making short sallies low over the sand to catch flies and sand-hoppers.

Best time to see: All year round with a spring peak in March and an autumn peak in October. Note that the White Wagtail is not seen in the winter months.

Numbers: Usually in ones and twos spread along the beach. Has started to breed here but at present only one or two pairs.

Wren

This **very small** bird is seen everywhere with its **cocked tail** and brown plumage. Will often perch out in the open to scold you with its churring call and has a long song which after a few short introductory notes will always include the long dry *'trrrrrrrrrr'* call.

Best place to see: Everywhere, but especially on gorse bushes and hedgerows.

Best time to see: All year round.

Numbers: Despite being our commonest land-bird with an estimated breeding population of between 1500 and 3000 pairs it is usually only seen in ones and twos – but you see them all the time!

"I may be small but I'm also beautiful"

Dunnock

Another LBJ (little brown job) with a **strikingly dark brown** plumage and grey head. Has a very **thin bill** from which emanates its squeaky but pleasing warbling song – not unlike that of Wren but delivered more slowly.

Best place to see: In hedgerows and scrub on any of the islands.

Best time to see: All year round.

Numbers: Usually seen singly. However it is estimated that 500 or more pairs breed here, but they are widely distributed in suitable habitat and hence large concentrations are not seen together.

Robin

Look at any Christmas card. Although everyone knows a Robin has a **red breast** maybe not many of us have looked closely to see its grey head markings, or that the juvenile Robin has a speckled brown breast with no red whatsoever.

Best place to see: In hedgerows and vegetated areas on any island.

Best time to see: All year round.

Numbers: Usually seen singly. Around 250-300 pairs breed here, mainly on St Mary's and Tresco with very few pairs on St Agnes and almost none on Bryher and St Martin's. Why there is this bias is not known. Although thought of as a resident in mainland Britain Scilly occasionally gets large numbers of birds from the continent that pass through on migration. For example in spring 2004 almost 500 were seen along the beaches of St Agnes, St Mary's and St Martin's but most were gone the next day!

Black Redstart

A small smart **grey-black** bird with a red rear end and **shimmering red tail** ('start' is Old English for tail). Can appear like a Robin in behaviour with its upright stance and very similar size.

Best place to see: Often on vegetation and trees near beaches such as at Porthloo St Mary's where the tamarisk trees at the far end are a favoured spot. Also, especially in autumn, it can be seen in ploughed fields such as those near Normandy St Mary's.

Best time to see: Mainly passing through on migration in October, after which a few may remain to winter. A spring passage also occurs in March.

Numbers: Small groups of two to ten birds seen when on migration, with ones and twos being seen if they remain for the winter.

Stonechat

Often sits up conspicuously on isolated vegetation showing its rounded **black head** (male, see photo) and red suffusion on the chest. The **white collar** also shows up well. The female has a dark brown head with only the hint of a white collar and pale eyebrow. Has a **distinctive call**, often likened to two pebbles being rolled together – *'track-track'*.

Best place to see: Along the coastal edge of any island in low vegetation such as gorse, tall weeds and mallow.

Best time to see: All year round.

Numbers: Often a pair will be seen close together, the male on one bush making its call, the female watching some metres away from another bush. Just over 50 pairs breed on the islands.

Similar species: The *Whinchat* (page 123) is a migrant only and has a more strongly marked eyebrow.

Northern Wheatear

A robust bird, appearing larger than its actual size, often **standing up conspicuously** on low lying stones or vegetation. The male is beautifully marked with a **black highwayman's mask**, a **grey back** and darker, almost black, wings. The female is similar but less bright.

Best place to see: Close to the coast on low grass and heather. Good spots are Wingletang St Agnes and Peninnis St Mary's. Also frequents sandy beaches keeping to the top of the beach where rocks and seaweed abound.

Best time to see: Spring passage from mid-March to early June; autumn passage from August to October.

Numbers: Spread out over the heather, single birds will be seen at regular intervals. You could easily see 20-30 on a spring day whilst walking across Wingletang St Agnes. One or two pairs have bred in recent years.

Ring Ouzel

A Blackbird with a **white breast plate** – that's the Ring Ouzel. Closer inspection will also show pale edges to the body feathers, called fringing.

Best place to see: A variety of habitats ranging from ploughed fields to hedgerows, or on beaches.

Best time to see: Autumn passage in mid-October with a smaller spring passage in April.

Numbers: From one to three birds is typical.

Blackbird

A medium size woodland bird with **black** (male) and **dark brown** (female) plumage. Birds in Scilly have a more **orange** coloured bill to birds on mainland, sometimes red (see opposite). However that does NOT make them a Chough which is much larger (nearer to a Crow), has a down-curved bill and is *extremely* rare.

Best place to see: On all main islands in woodland, along hedgerows and in ploughed fields.

Best time to see: All year round.

Numbers: From one to ten birds may be seen feeding in a field, but as you walk around that sort of number will be seen in many places. There are about 500 pairs breeding in Scilly.

"Oh! What a beautiful morning!"

Fieldfare

A large winter thrush with a striking **grey head and neck**. Closer examination will show the **white eyebrow**, the cold reddish-brown back and blotches on the breast and flanks. A distinctive bird.

Best place to see: On open grassy areas such as Carn Gwaval School St Mary's playing field. Also likes ploughed earthy fields, where it feeds in the furrows.

Best time to see: Birds fly to Britain for the winter with some getting down to the far south-west by mid-October. Most feed and continue on, but a few will over-winter through to March.

Numbers: Sometimes 10-15 can be seen feeding in the open, often accompanied by Redwings and other thrushes. Large groups of 40 or more are not uncommon.

Redwing

A **dapper** thrush with its **white eyebrow** and **red flash** on the flanks (and underwing, when seen in flight).

Best place to see: Similar to Fieldfare, feeding on grassy areas such as school playing fields.

Best time to see: From mid-October through to March.

Numbers: Sometimes 30 or more can be seen feeding in the open, often with Fieldfare and other thrushes. Larger groups of up to 100 birds are possible.

Song Thrush

The standard thrush with **brown back**, and dark spots on an off-white underside. Seeing them so closely (and seemingly quite large) some people assume they must be Mistle Thrush but that species is *very rare* in Scilly.

Best place to see: Just about anywhere – in hedgerows, ploughed fields, woodland, walking down Hugh Street and even sitting on rocky outcrops. They often come into houses – especially if fed with Co-op currants!

Best time to see: Any time.

Numbers: Usually in ones and twos, with groups of up to 20 when feeding in the countryside. With well over 500 pairs breeding here, the density of Song Thrush in Scilly is TEN TIMES that on mainland Britain. This is probably due to the amount of insects produced by the islands' non-chemical, and non-intensive farming.

"I've always been an early riser!"

Sedge Warbler

A **sandy brown** small warbler, with a striking **white eyebrow**. Has a scratchy song which has no rhythm, and includes a variety of trills, squeaks and scratches.

Best place to see: In reed beds around freshwater pools such as at Lower and Higher Moors St Mary's. Also in the small sallows and low scrub within, and close to, those reed beds.

Best time to see: Summer, from late April through to October.

Numbers: Usually a single bird is seen clinging to a reed or perched high in the bush. About 10 pairs breed on the islands.

Reed Warbler

A **warm buff** coloured small warbler, with **no distinctive markings**. Spiky bill. Has a monotonous scratchy song but, unlike Sedge Warbler, this one can be conducted, as phrases are rhythmical and often repeated.

Best place to see: In reed beds around freshwater pools such as at Lower and Higher Moors St Mary's. In summer it is less likely than Sedge Warbler to be seen in bushes, but on passage in autumn it will be seen foraging in scrub and similar habitat.

Best time to see: Summer, from mid-April through to the end of October.

Numbers: Usually a single bird, sometimes two close together. About 20 pairs breed on the islands.

Blackcap

A small warbler with **grey plumage** and **black** head (male) or **chestnut brown** head (female).

Best place to see: Woodland and hedgerows.

Best time to see: Mainly in autumn but with our warmer winters a few now winter here.

Numbers: Usually a single bird, or in pairs during summer and early autumn. Between three and ten pairs breed here, although this may increase as over-wintering birds could stay on to breed.

Common Whitethroat

A small warbler with grey-brown back and rusty coloured wings. The **grey head** is off-set by the **white throat**. It has a chattering song, and may hop out to scold you with an aggressive *'churrr'*.

Best place to see: Mainly in bushes, hedgerows, brambles and scrub.

Best time to see: From mid-April through to mid-October

Numbers: Usually just one bird.

Common Chiffchaff

A small warbler that is easily confused with Willow Warbler (see opposite). Chiffchaff has a dusky **grey-green** plumage, and a paler throat and belly, with a diffused pale yellow eyebrow. The legs are black. It has a distinctive repeating 'chiff-chaff' song.

Best place to see: Woodland and hedgerows.

Best time to see: Mainly in autumn, but with our warmer winters in the last couple of decades, a few now winter here and some stay on to breed.

Numbers: Generally seen in ones and twos. About 25 pairs breed on the islands.

Willow Warbler

A small warbler that is easily confused with Chiffchaff (see opposite). Willow Warbler is usually the brighter with a **grey-green** plumage, a **lemon yellow throat** and paler belly, with a clearly marked pale yellow eyebrow. The legs are pale brown. Its song is a melodious descending trill, each note clearly sung *'pheww trilly trilly, pheww trilly trilly, pheww pheww pheww phuuuu'* – the last 4 notes dropping rapidly away.

Best place to see: Woodland and hedgerows.

Best time to see: Mainly in spring from mid-March to early May and again in autumn during August and September.

Numbers: Generally seen in ones and twos. Between 10 and 20 pairs breed on the islands.

Goldcrest

Britain's **smallest** bird, along with Firecrest. Has a bright **gold crown stripe** on a round face with hardly any neck, and a small black eye. Often reveals its presence by a thin **three note call** *'see-see-see'* but seeing the bird can be a lot more difficult as it flits restlessly through the pines.

Best place to see: Woodland especially pine belts such as around the north end of St Mary's, above Middle Town St Martin's and on the east side of Tresco. Another favourite spot is Abbey Drive Tresco.

Best time to see: Late autumn passage starts from October, and a fair number remain over the winter period.

Numbers: Small flocks will pass through the trees on a foraging trip, maybe numbering up to 10 birds. About 20 pairs breed here.

Firecrest

A gem of a bird with its **boldly striped head** – yellow, black and white stripes abound (see photo). The broad **white eyebrow** marks it out from Goldcrest and it also shows an olive-bronze wash on the shoulders.

Best place to see: Woodland and hedgerows.

Best time to see: October to the end of March.

Numbers: Usually just a single bird. This is a scarce bird in Britain but Scilly is one of the best places to see one.

Spotted Flycatcher

A fairly **nondescript** small woodland bird with grey-brown plumage and a **prominent black eye** set in a plain face. Sits very upright on a protruding branch before sallying off to catch an insect, often returning to the same perch.

Best place to see: The edges of woodland or on dead trees such as around the pine belt on Garrison St Mary's.

Best time to see: Highest numbers are in September but it is present from May to October.

Numbers: Usually only a single bird is seen. One pair has bred here in recent years.

Pied Flycatcher

A **black and white** woodland bird in the male; the female (see photo) is more subdued. The black head and prominent **white flash** in the wing will catch the eye as it sits on a branch looking out for its flying insect prey. Normally returns to a different perch (compare with Spotted Flycatcher).
Best place to see: Woodland glades and the edges of hedgerows, especially where sunlit.
Best time to see: August and September. Also in spring, mid-April to mid-May, when in pristine breeding plumage.
Numbers: Usually a single bird is seen.

Blue Tit

Blue crown, blue wings, white cheeks and **lemon yellow body** make this one of Britain's brightest and most obvious birds. Often picked up by its jittery flight songs – *'chee-dee-dee-dee'* and *'pee-zee-tzay'* amongst others.

Best place to see: Woodlands and hedgerows.

Best time to see: All year round.

Numbers: Ones and twos and sometimes in small roving tit flocks of up to 10 or more birds. Between 50 and 75 pairs breed on the islands, with St Mary's being the stronghold. Surprisingly Tresco, with all its woodland, only has a few pairs and there is the occasional pair on St Agnes and St Martin's.

Great Tit

Prominent **black head** with white cheeks and a **bright yellow body**, with a black line down the centre of the breast, serve to make the Great Tit an easily identified bird. Has a distinctive see-sawing two-note song *'twee-cherr', twee-cherr'* repeated often.

Best place to see: Woodlands and hedgerows.

Best time to see: All year round.

Numbers: Usually in ones and twos. About 100 pairs breed across the inhabited islands and they are much more widely spread than Blue Tit.

Jackdaw

The smallest member of the crow family with a **grey nape** and, when seen well, a white eye.

Best place to see: Flying over well wooded areas, so Tresco is the favoured island.

Best time to see: All year round.

Numbers: Had been a very rare bird in Scilly but in 1983 a massive flock of 4000 or more birds flew over. A similar event but on a smaller scale (about 500 birds) took place in 1990 and some of these remained, giving rise to the first breeding record in 1992. Presumably the off-spring of this pair has led to Jackdaws still being seen around the islands in ones and twos, and it is hoped that further breeding will occur.

Raven

The largest of the crows, slightly **larger than a Buzzard**, with all-black plumage and a distinctive long **diamond-shaped tail.** Its call is a very deep metallic *'cronk-cronk'*.

Best place to see: Over the Eastern Isles and around St Martin's.

Best time to see: All year round.

Numbers: A pair has bred on Eastern Isles for a few years and can be seen with one or two young through the summer and up to September. It is thought that another pair bred on Rosevear in 2005.

Carrion Crow

A large **all-black bird** of the crow family; it even has a black bill.

The Hooded Crow, which is now recognised as a separate species, is seen in Scilly and has a very pale mantle (upper back) and pale under belly. However 'Hoodies' have inter-bred with Carrion Crows and so odd looking hybrids are seen, usually favouring Tresco heliport.

Best place to see: In farmland and on beaches. A favoured spot is up-country on St Mary's and on the sandy beaches near Pelistry St Mary's.

Best time to see: All year round.

Numbers: Apart from one or two flying overhead you will often see flocks of 10 to 20 birds in fields or on beaches. About 10-15 pairs breed here.

Starling

If you look closely the Starling is a lot more beautiful than many people think, with its **iridescent green black** plumage and bright yellow spiky bill. Also its song is unique with lots of clicks, trills and scratches, hardly anything being repeated and it also includes much mimicry – not just of other birds but of phone rings and the like. It has a distinctive 'flying triangle' shape in flight.

Best place to see: Anywhere, with known congregations in Hugh Town and up-country near Pelistry St Mary's.

Best time to see: All year round.

Numbers: Often in flocks of 10-30 birds and up to 100 birds are not uncommon. Between 250 and 500 pairs breed here.

House Sparrow

Still a common bird in Scilly with its well known **chirpy call**. Basically fairly drab although the male (see photo) sports a **grey crown**, white cheeks and a **black bib**.
Best place to see: Around human habitation, so Hugh Town St Mary's and the small built-up areas at New Grimsby Tresco. Also cultivated fields are used by House Sparrow flocks, so up-country St Mary's and Borough Farm Tresco are good spots.
Best time to see: All year round.
Numbers: Flocks of up to 100 birds are not uncommon. About 500 pairs breed here with one favoured location being the Garrison Walls St Mary's, going up through Sally Port.

Chaffinch

A small bird with a pink-red chest, **grey head** and with prominent **flashes of white** in the wing (male, see photo). The female is duller in colour. Has a distinctive metallic *'spink spink'* call.

Best place to see: Hedgerows, woodland and small trees and sallows anywhere. Also in ploughed fields.

Best time to see: All year round, although in summer it is very rare on St Martin's Bryher and St Agnes.

Numbers: Usually seen in ones and twos, with small feeding flocks occurring in ploughed fields. About 50 pairs breed here.

Similar species: The *Brambling* (page 123), which only occurs as a migrant passing through the islands, could lead to confusion.

Greenfinch

Quite large for a finch with an **olive-green back** and **yellow flash** in the wing. Gives a long drawn out nasal *'dweezzzz'* call, often from an exposed perch.

Best place to see: Hedgerows, woodland and small trees and sallows anywhere.

Best time to see: All year round with a peak during October as migrants pass through.

Numbers: Usually seen as single birds or in small flocks of up to five birds. Between 100 and 150 pairs breed here.

Goldfinch

What colours! A **red face**, **white cheeks** and black crown (see photo) are complemented (?!) by black wings with a bright **yellow flash**. Who says British birds are boring compared to those jungle exotics?

Best place to see: Often seen on plant heads where crops have been allowed to go to seed. Also in hedgerows where they fly off in front of you as you approach.

Best time to see: Mainly between April and October, especially during the summer breeding season, although a few birds are seen in other months.

Numbers: Small groups of 5-20 birds feeding on seed heads. Between 50 and 100 pairs breed here.

Siskin

A smart **little** bird, the male having complex **yellow, olive and black** markings and a black and yellow face pattern. The female (see photo) is the same but duller, without such a distinctive face.

Best place to see: Wooded areas on any island.

Best time to see: October without a doubt.

Numbers: Flocks flying overhead will often number from 30 to 100 birds or more.

Linnet

A pair of birds flying away from you, low over the gorse, with a soft **twittering call** and showing flashes of white in the tail? They were Linnets. Seen well the male has a bright **red chest**, the female is duller.

Best place to see: Spread over scrub and heathland such as Peninnis St Mary's, Wingletang St Agnes or The Plains St Martin's.

Best time to see: From March through to October – very scarce in the winter months.

Numbers: Often seen in pairs, but with many such pairs likely to be encountered in one area. Around 500 pairs breed here.

SIMILAR SPECIES

WHOOPER SWAN – Larger than *Mute Swan*, with a **yellow bill at the base**, and a black tip – the reverse colour pattern to *Mute Swan*. Only occurs in winter, from late October through to March.

WHITE-FRONTED GOOSE – Smaller than *Canada Goose*, with a generally grey-brown plumage, a **white shield** at the base of the bill, and **black streaks** on the belly. Only occurs in winter, usually from October through to February.

BRENT GOOSE – Even smaller than *White-fronted Goose* (above) with a grey plumage, **black head and neck** with a small white chin mark, much smaller than that of *Canada Goose*. More likely to be found **swimming on the sea** than other geese. Seen at any time of year but very unlikely from June to August.

GREAT SHEARWATER – A medium to large shearwater, gliding on stiff wings **close to the waves**. Note the **dark brown cap**, separated from the grey back by a **white collar**. Most likely from a pelagic (see page 4) in August.

MERLIN – Britain's **smallest bird of prey**. Generally a grey plumage (browner in the female) although this is often difficult to see as it dashes past you in its **very fast flight**. Pointed wings, often swept back, with **square-ended tail**. Can be seen all year round except June, July and August.

LITTLE RINGED PLOVER – Its body is longer than *Ringed Plover* and it has a **yellow eye-ring**, quite obvious when you look for it! The **all black bill** is finer than a Ringed Plover's. Occurs in April, May and September.

GREY PLOVER – Like a *Golden Plover* but with a **spangled grey-black and white** plumage. In flight it has a diagnostic feature: black 'arm-pits'. Most likely from mid-September through the winter up to mid-April.

BAR-TAILED GODWIT – A large brown wader with **long bill** (basically straight but very **slightly upturned**). Long **black legs**. Plumage varies between summer, when at its most red, through to winter when it is greyer. Most likely from mid-April to May and then from mid-August to October.

GREEN SANDPIPER – A medium sized wader that has been '**dipped in a pot of white paint**'. The back is very dark green, divided by a sharp line to the white belly. In flight its **white rump** stands out. Most likely seen from mid-July to the end of September and also on spring migration, in April.

WOOD SANDPIPER – Similar to *Green Sandpiper* but just **not as contrasting**. The plumage is brown, and the demarcation between back and belly is **far more graduated**, whilst in flight the white rump is not as distinct. Best seen from August to mid-September.

ARCTIC TERN – Very similar to Common Tern but **bill is crimson** rather than bright red, and the **tail streamers** are much longer. It is not easy to distinguish these two species but in Scilly the *Common Tern* is aptly named outnumbering the Arctic by about 100:1. Occurs from April to October.

LITTLE AUK – A **very small** Auk, about the size of a Starling, usually seen sitting on the sea with its black back and almost negligible **stubby bill**. Occurs in winter, from October through to March.

YELLOW WAGTAIL – Like the *Grey Wagtail* but the back is **greenish yellow** and the tail is not as long. The underside is completely yellow whilst its congener has a white area in the middle of the belly. Seen late April and first week in May, then from the last week of August to October.

WHINCHAT – Similar to *Stonechat* but has a **white eyebrow** and white moustache, still apparent, although much duller, on females. Only occurs on migration between mid-April and mid-May and then from August to October.

BRAMBLING – The female is very like a *Chaffinch* but the male with its **black head**, **orange breast** and wing-flash is quite distinctive. In flight it shows a white rump. Occurs mainly from mid-October to the end of November, and a smaller spring passage from late April to first week in May.

Rare Species

RING-NECKED DUCK – A medium sized duck with iridescent upper parts, a **peaked head** and long bill with **white ring**. The staring yellow eye is distinctive. Birds have been seen on Great Pool Tresco and Porth Hellick Pool St Mary's in recent years.

PECTORAL SANDPIPER – In Scilly, the commonest visitor from America. A nondescript medium sized brown wader with a sharply **demarcated breast** (the pectoral band of its name). Has a slightly down-curved bill. Most likely from mid-August to the end of September.

WRYNECK – An extraordinary bird with **cryptic plumage**. Smaller than a Song Thrush it can be found **creeping** along coastal paths, or in hedges, feeding on ants. Has an undulating flight, sometimes gliding long distances. Gets its name from its ability to turn its head almost backwards. The best month to see Wryneck is September.

WOODCHAT SHRIKE – Often sits up on a **prominent perch** looking for its insect prey. The **rusty brown head**, highwayman's **mask** and white belly stand out. Most likely to occur in May.

ROSY STARLING – A visitor from south-east Europe and central Asia. Unmistakeable in its breeding plumage (see photo) with **pink shawl and breast**, but immatures, which are more likely, are a boring washed-out **pale brown** – the Fawn Yawn. Any time of year, but most likely in autumn.

COMMON CROSSBILL – A **dumpy** bird with (you've guessed it!) a **crossed bill** which is used to get kernels out of pine cones. The male is bright red, the female sage green but colours can vary. Often comes to pools to drink after feeding. Most likely in July, August or September.

ORTOLAN BUNTING – Rare nationally but regular in Scilly with usually two or three each year, normally in September and early October. An LBJ (little brown job) except for its prominent **cream moustache** and **pale eye-ring**.

Check List and Index